THIS ADULT COLORING BOOK CONTAINS A VAST COLLECTION OF 50 SWEAR WORDS IN COOL DOODLES THAT WILL HELP YOU WITH HOURS OF STRESS RELIEF THROUGH CREATIVE EXPRESSIONS. ILLUSTRATIONS HAVE A COMPLEXITY LEVEL FROM ROOKIE TO EXPERT LEVELS.

# FUCKING PIECE OF SHIT

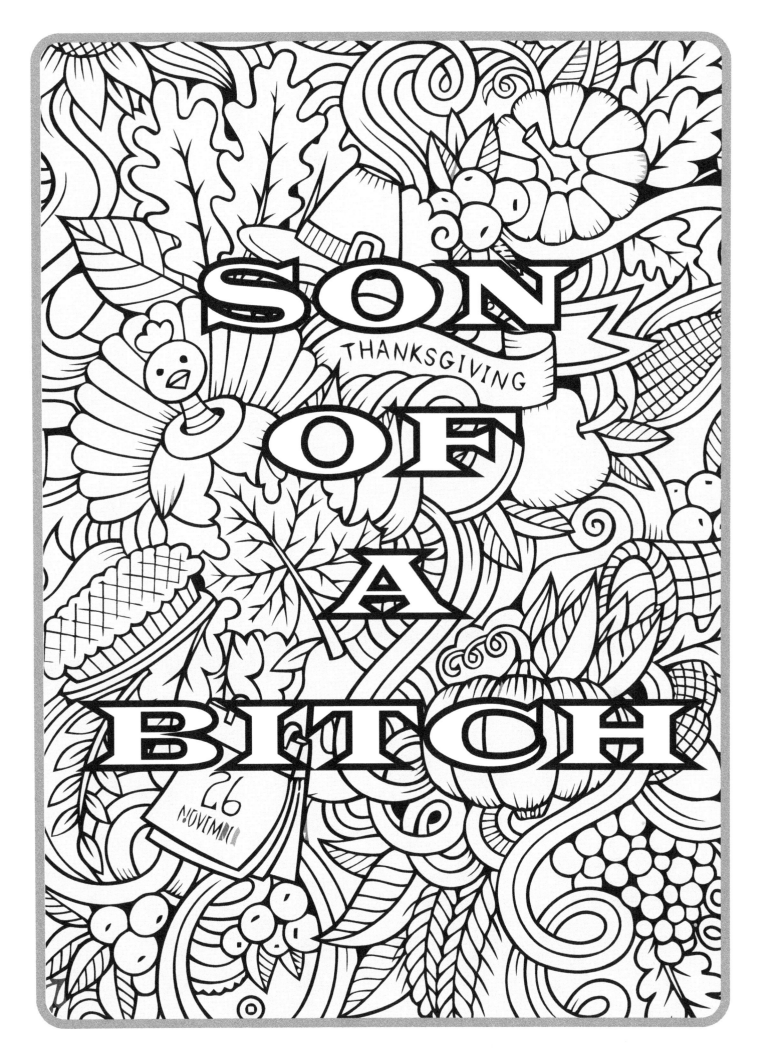

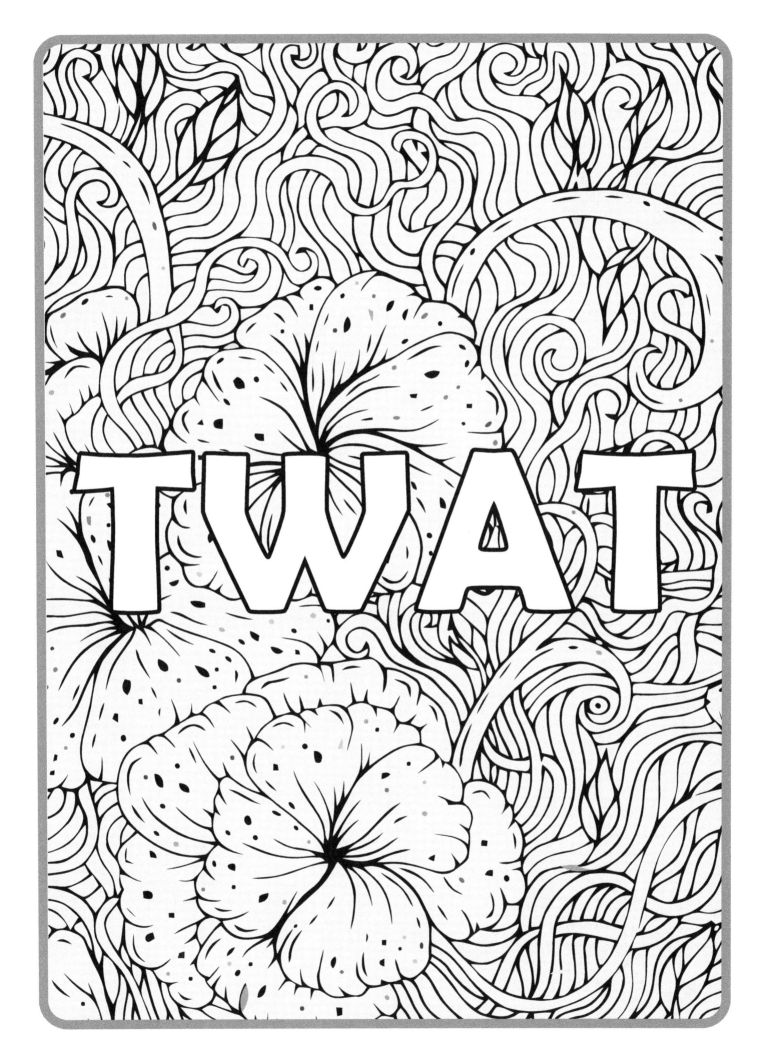

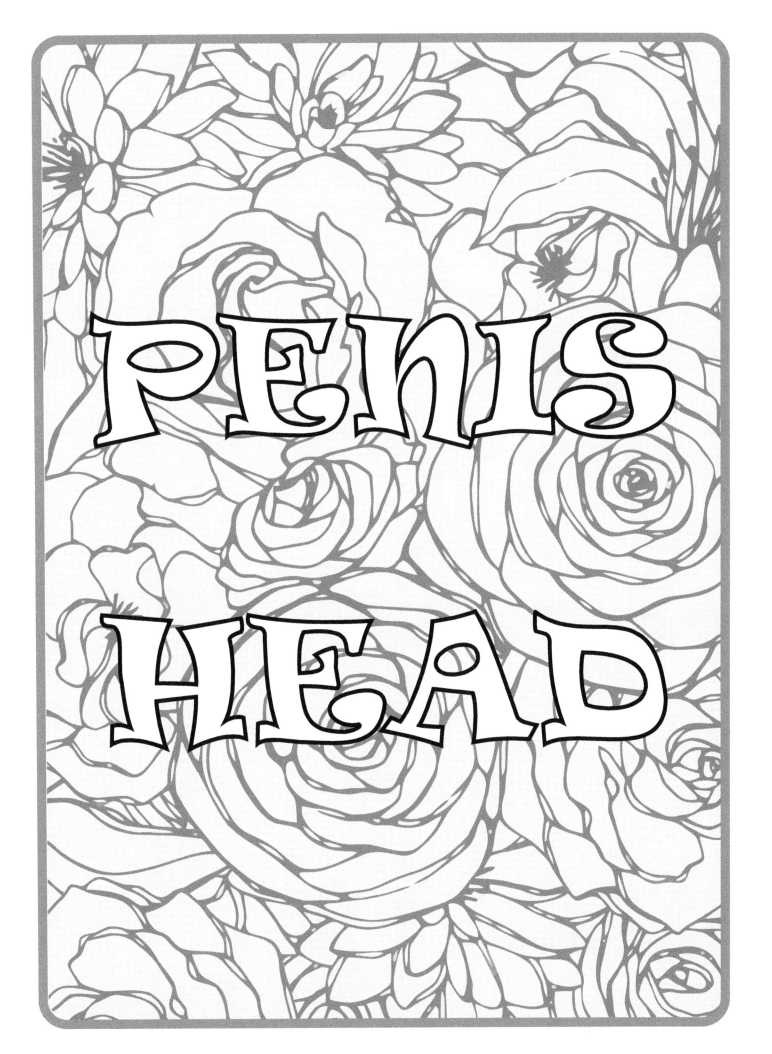

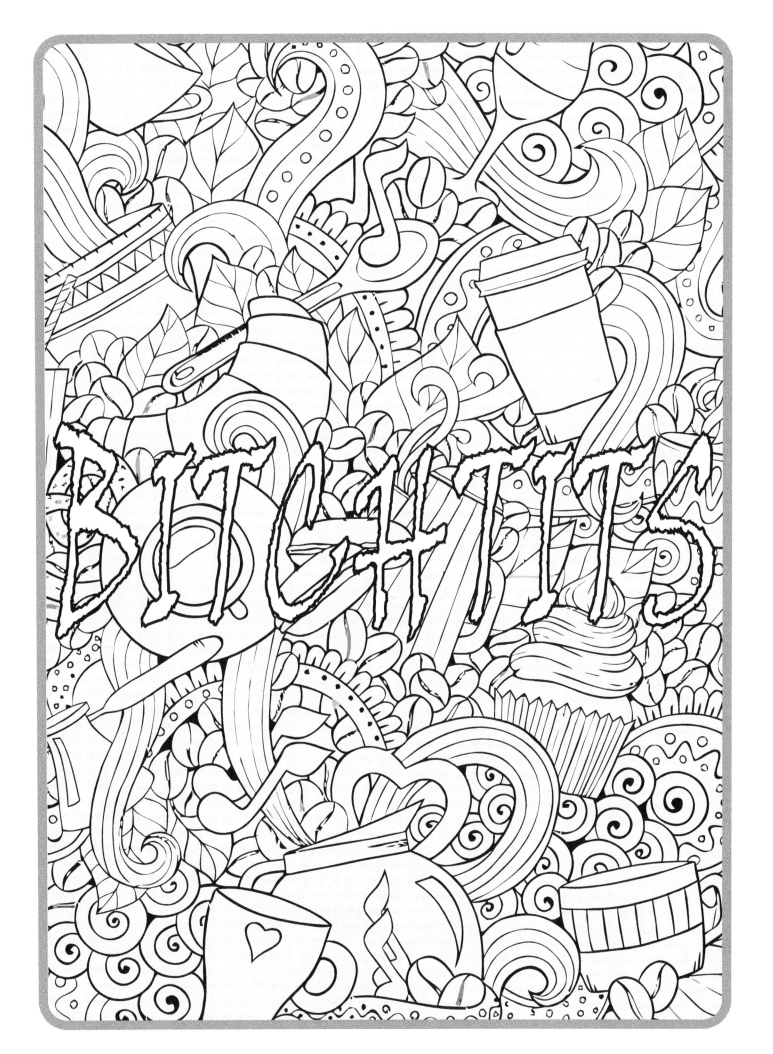

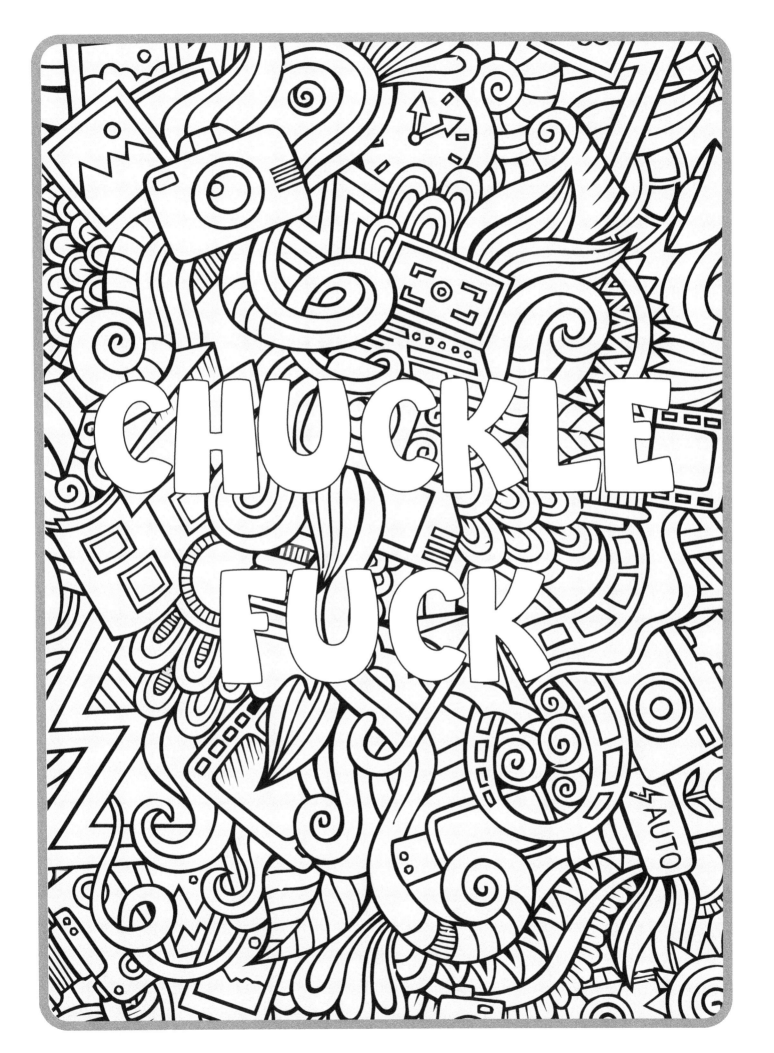

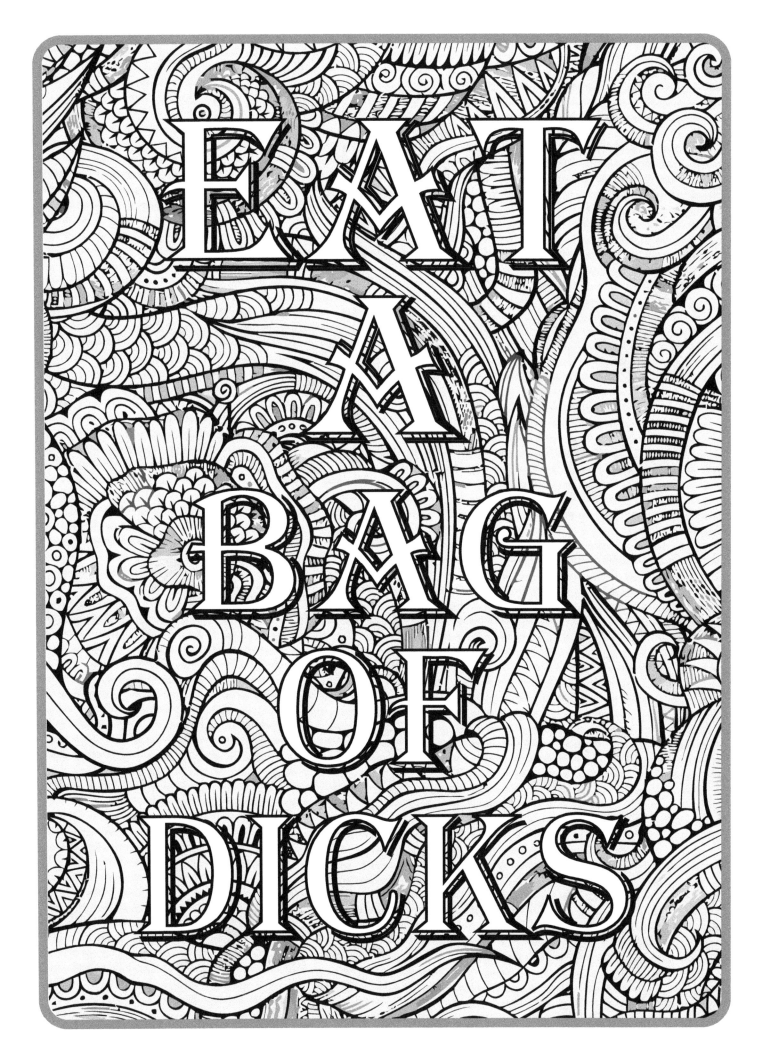

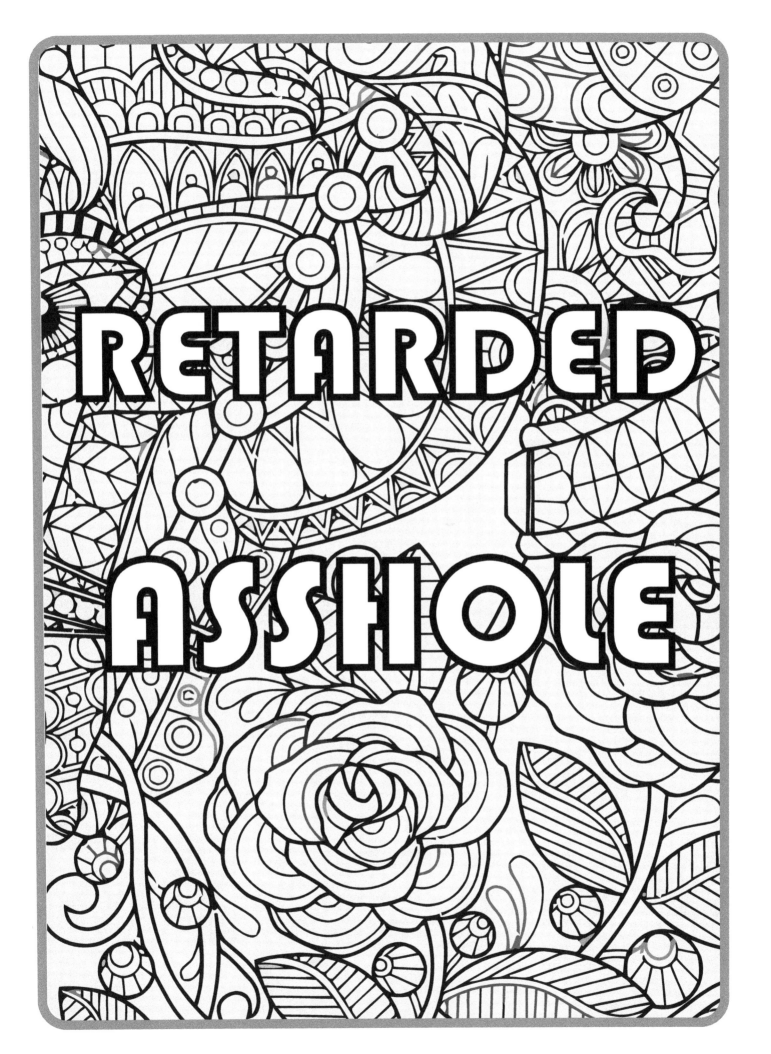

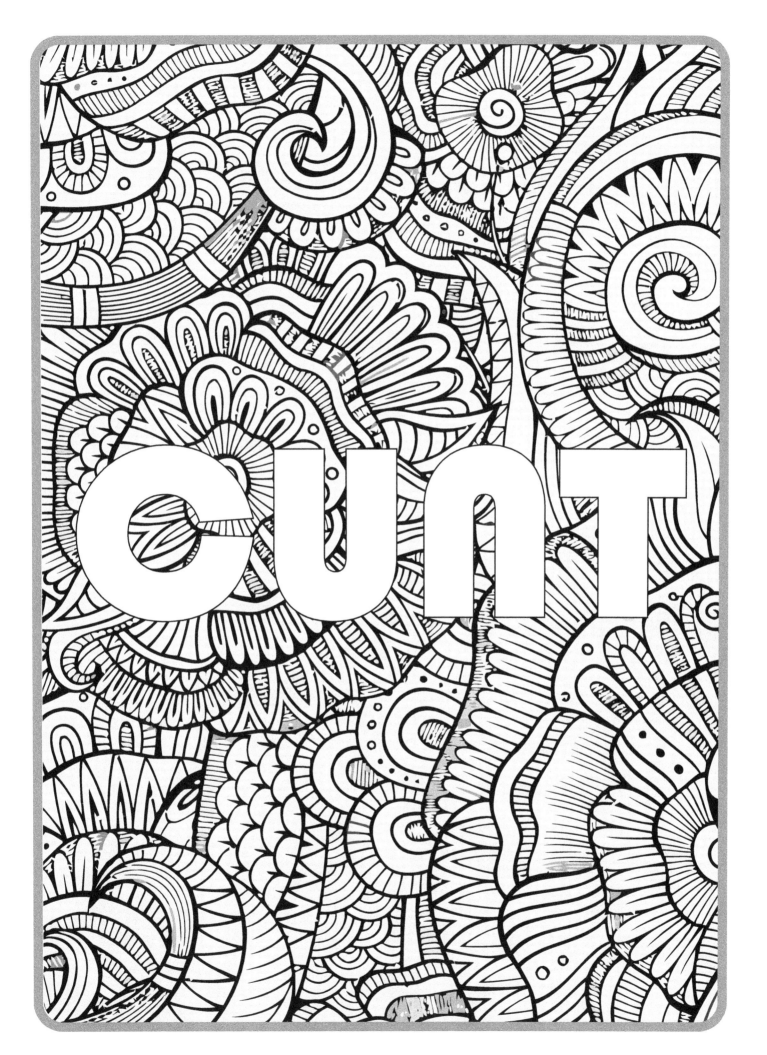

www.ingramcontent.com/pod-product-compliance
Lightning Source LLC
Chambersburg PA
CBHW081037160225
22036CB00032B/1030